My Science Library

Our Sun Brings Life

by Conrad J. Storad

Science Content Editor:
Kristi Lew

ROURKE CLASSROOM
www.rourkeclassroom.com

Science content editor: Kristi Lew
A former high school teacher with a background in biochemistry and more than 10 years of experience in cytogenetic laboratories, Kristi Lew specializes in taking complex scientific information and making it fun and interesting for scientists and non-scientists alike. She is the author of more than 20 science books for children and teachers.

www.rourkeclassroom.com

Photo credits:
Cover © Carlos Caetano, Mitar Vidakovic; Cover logo frog © Eric Pohl, test tube © Sergey Lazarev; Page 3 © happydancing; Page 5 © Yuriy Kulyk; Page 7 © BirDiGoL; Page 9 © Heizel; Page 11 © vovan; Page 13 © nadiya_sergey; Page 15 © Andrejs Pidjass; Page 17 © Andriano; Page 19 © Lori Skelton; Page 20 © Dolly; Page 22 © Lori Skelton, BirDiGoL, happydancing; Page 23 © Yuriy Kulyk, Andrejs Pidjass, Heizel

Editor: Kelli Hicks

My Science Library series produced for Rourke by Blue Door Publishing, Florida

Library of Congress Cataloging-in-Publication Data

Storad, Conrad J.
 Our sun brings life / Conrad J. Storad.
    p. cm. -- (My science library)
 Includes bibliographical references and index.
 ISBN 978-1-61741-723-8 (Hard cover) (alk. paper)
 ISBN 978-1-61741-925-6 (Soft cover)
 1. Sunshine--Juvenile literature. 2. Sun--Juvenile literature. I. Title.
 QC911.2.S76 2011
 523.7--dc22
                            2011003761

Rourke Publishing
Printed in China, Voion Industry
   Guangdong Province
042011
042011LP

ROURKE CLASSROOM

www.rourkeclassroom.com - rourke@rourkepublishing.com
Post Office Box 643328 Vero Beach, Florida 32964

Have you ever seen a **star**?

Look at the **sky**.
Our **Sun** is a star.

5

It is the only star you can see in the day.

The Sun is big.
It is bigger than **Earth**.

Sun

Earth

Our Sun lights the sky each day.

Our Sun makes the Earth's air, **water**, and land warm for all living things.

Sunlight helps plants
make food.

Some plants are food
for animals and people.

Fruits and vegetables are some of the foods we get from plants.

There would be no life on Earth without the Sun.

SHOW what you know

1. Where can you see a star?

2. Why is our Sun important?

3. How does the Sun help plants?

Picture Glossary

Earth (URTH):
The planet on which we live is called Earth.

fruits (FROOTS):
Fruits are the juicy, fleshy parts of plants. They contain a seed or seeds.

sky (SKI):
The sky is the place between the Earth and outer space.

star (STAAR):
A star is a mass of burning gas seen in the night sky. Stars are far, far away from our world.

Sun (SUN):
The Sun is the star closest to our world. It is the only star we can see during the day.

water (WAW-TER):
Water is the clear liquid that falls from the sky. Lakes, rivers, and oceans are filled with water.

Index

Websites

www.nasa.gov/audience/forkids/kidsclub/flash/

www.kids.nineplanets.org/portfoli.htm

www.kidsastronomy.com/our_sun.htm

About the Author

Conrad J. Storad is the award-winning author of more than 30 books for young readers. He writes about animals, creepy crawlers, and planets. He was a magazine editor at Arizona State University for 25 years. Conrad lives in Tempe, Arizona with his wife Laurie and their miniature wiener dog, Sophia.